A Week on

GW01313738

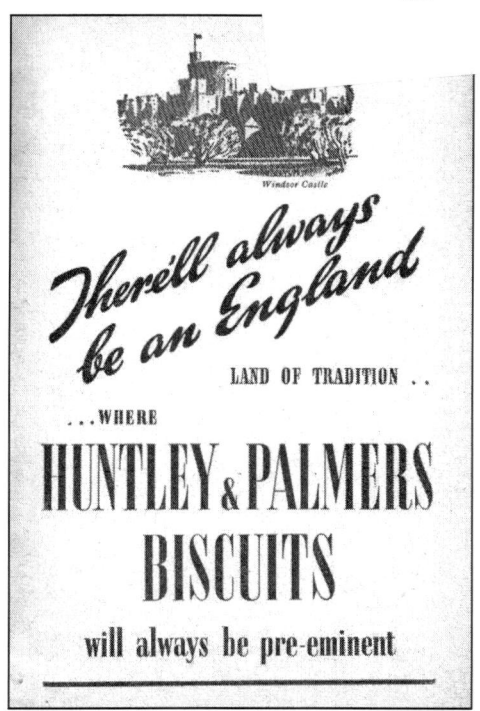

Windsor Castle

There'll always be an England

LAND OF TRADITION . .

. . . WHERE

HUNTLEY & PALMERS
BISCUITS

will always be pre-eminent

Introduction

I am Karen and live with my husband Bret and our cat Bosun on our Dutch Barge on the River Thames. We travel most days, generally through Oxfordshire and Berkshire, stopping where the fancy takes us.

About three years ago we started what we thought would be a harmless hobby as World War II Home Front re-enactors, but like many hobbies it has become quite an obsession.

We only focus on the war years and only Home Front, so in other words what life was like for ordinary folk in this country during the war. As well as going to 1940s events with our various displays we do talks to groups, young and old, and spend an extraordinary amount of time researching, adding to our collection of memorabilia and creating replicas.

If you are particularly interested in what we do and where we are doing it please take a look at our website www.doingtheirbit.co.uk.

Our interest in food rationing stems from the food itself, I love cooking it and Bret loves eating it, a perfect combination.

One wet Sunday in October we sat watching the rain drip down the windows and wondered what it would be like to live on rations. Would we starve and head to the nearest chip shop? Would we loathe the food and swear never again? How hard could it really be?

Our research and experience led to us writing this book so that others may be encouraged to try it. This is not a recipe book, nor is it a history book, but I hope a combination of both which will entertain, educate and inspire you.

 The information taken for this book is from original 1940s publications and one which has been particularly useful is Food Facts for the Kitchen Front. There is no date of publication, but I think it is fair to assume it is early war when the Ministry of Food were really pushing home food values and nutrition.

The foreword is by Lord Woolton, the Minister of Food, and is particularly good. I could not sum this up as well and eloquently as he, so here it is:

I should not care to present a copy of this book to the ghost of Mrs. Beeton. That generous phantom would no doubt be shocked by the simplicity of the recipes given here. It is a plain production; a war-time production pure and simple. The ingredients are pure and the methods of preparing them are simple.

But there is more to it than that. It is not a collection of makeshifts. Its lessons in cookery and food-values hold good for times of peace and plenty.

Publishers frequently express hopes that their new masterpieces will go down to prosperity.

3

It is good to think that prosperity will learn from those who had to cater and cook in Britain's front line.

Not long ago, in a grocer's, I overheard a conversation between two women shopping at the counter. One said to the other, "After all, housewives are war-workers same as anybody else, aren't they?"

They are. And that is why I can present this book to them. I hope that they will find it a serviceable weapon.

Woolton

A Bit of History

I thought it might be useful to start off with a little bit of history about rationing, which might explain and make more sense about what we did and why rationing was so necessary during the war.

Why was rationing necessary?

The answer to this question stems back to World War I and the depression that followed in the early 1920s. During the Great War much of our home-grown food was sent over to France to feed our boys fighting in the trenches.

A huge amount of our food was imported from abroad by the Merchant Navy and it became the task of the German U-boats to sink our merchant ships.

> Point of interest: U-boats were the anglicised name of the German Unterseeboot – literally meaning under-sea boat, which we call 'submarines'.

Added to this, our farmers and their horses went off to fight the Hun and the Women's Land Army tried with all their might to keep our farms going. The WLA was formed in 1917, and over 200,000 women worked the land along with 30,000 prisoners of war during WW1.

In 1916 the country was desperately in need of food, crops failed and in fact we only had six weeks of wheat left in the country. In these desperate times the Ministry of Food was formed to try to alleviate the situation, but was disbanded in 1921 when it was deemed no longer necessary.

After the Great War there followed a period of depression in the 1920s and the price of food shot up, meaning that the rich had plenty to eat and the poor could barely afford basic foods, leading to malnutrition and many health problems.

The lead-up to WW2

In 1935 with Germany's air force expansion and Hitler's introduction of mass conscription, the British Government had no choice but to think seriously about the problem of feeding the nation as war became inevitable.

Extensive research was carried out into nutrition and early in 1939 the Ministry of Food was formed again, led by nutritionist Sir Jack Drummond and the Minister, Lord Woolton. They were determined to educate the public about nutrition and put in place measures to feed the nation. The primary task of the Ministry was to ensure there was a fair and equal share of food for all, rich and poor alike.

Just after the outbreak of war the Government carried out the 1939 Register. This was a type of census to gather information about every man, woman and child living at each address. It was used for two purposes, first to issue identity cards and secondly to help with the production and distribution of ration books.

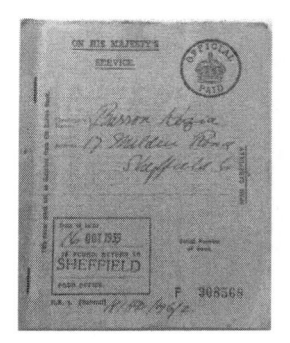 On 8th September 1939, just 5 days after war was declared, every person in the UK was issued with a ration book, even the royal family, although food rationing did not start until four months later on 8th January 1940.

There were different types of ration books. Most adults got the buff coloured one. Green was for pregnant women and those breast feeding, also for children under the age of 5, this included an extra milk ration. The blue one was for children aged 5-16, also including extra milk.

There was also another ration book for travellers. These were people whose jobs took them around the country and could not register with one particular shop. Interestingly the royal family were issued with travellers' ration books as they would be travelling around the country doing their 'job'.

Vegetarians, nursing mothers, pregnant women, children and some disabled (or 'physically defective' as they were called, no political correctness back then) got a double ration of cheese, another egg per week and more milk.

At the start of WWII Britain was importing 20 million tons of food per year. Hitler's first plan was to starve Britain into surrender, he thought that by cutting off our food supplies our little island would have no alternative but to bow to the mighty German army. How he underestimated us!

The German U-boats set out with a vengeance to destroy the Merchant Navy convoys, but the Government, and particularly the Ministry of Food, was prepared this time. Lessons learnt from WW1 and the subsequent depression meant they were ready and plans had been put into place.

How did rationing work?

Firstly, housewives registered with local shops such as butchers and grocers. There were no supermarkets then, just small individual shops.

You could not turn up at any shop and buy goods. Ration books were presented, and the shop keeper stamped or wrote his name in the front of the ration book against the rationed items to be purchased.

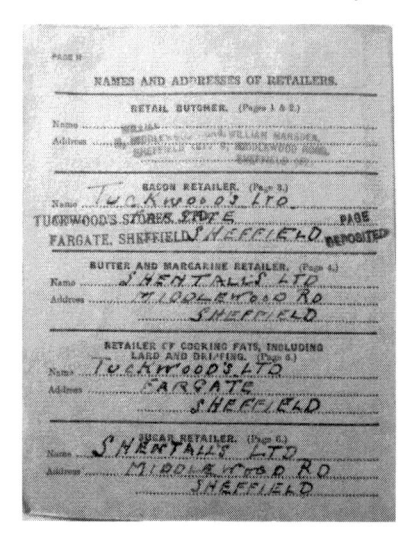

Each week the housewife would take her ration book, and those of the people living with her, to the shop, the coupons would be cut out or stamped and she would be permitted to buy the goods.

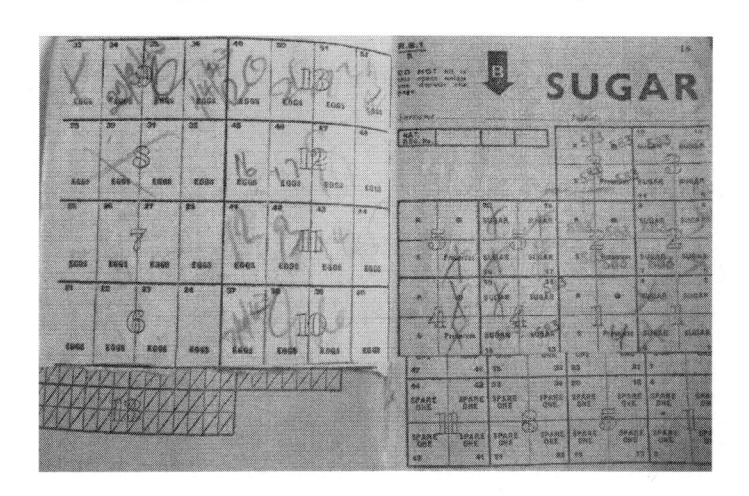

This sounds simple, but in reality there were often large queues, particularly at the butchers, and when you got to the front of the queue you would be lucky to get whatever was left.

In WW1 shopkeepers could charge whatever they wanted for food, but in WW2 the price of food was capped by the Government to stop unscrupulous shopkeepers from over-charging.

What food was rationed?

Not all food was rationed at the beginning of the war. Bacon or ham, butter and sugar were the first to be rationed.

These were shortly followed by meat, tea, jam, cheese, butter, lard, margarine, milk, breakfast cereals and eggs.

Although these were the items which were rationed other goods were often in short supply.

Weekly Rations for One Adult in 1940

Butter	2oz (57g)
Margarine	4oz (114g)
Cooking Fat	4oz (114g)
Eggs	Fresh: 1 per week
	Dried: 1 box every month
Bacon/Ham	4oz (114g)
Cheese	2oz (57g)
Milk	3 pints (1.7L) summer, 2 pints winter (1L)
Sugar	8oz (226g)
Meat	To the value of 1s 2d (about £1.70) for ½ lb (228g)
Jam	1 lb (454g) every month
Tea	2oz (57g)
Sweets	8oz (226g) every month

A few observations on the amount of food on ration and things to point out here.

On the face of it the amount of fats seems quite generous and at events I have heard people commenting that they would not use that much fat, but bear in mind that vegetable oil was rarely used, cooking fat comprised mainly of dripping and animal fats.

Secondly one fresh egg per week – well, we usually get through a couple of dozen a week with no problems so this must have been a real hardship.

Cheese, well what can I say? It's about the size of a small match box, the size that you would normally nibble on while cooking your evening meal.

Meat was sold by value, so you could get much more cheap stewing steak than fine fillet steak. A lot of careful and imaginative cooking had to be practiced to make the meat ration stretch.

Tea... 2oz. Although tea bags had been popular in the USA since the early 1930s, they were very slow to catch on in Britain and tea was sold loose. The tea leaves were used time and time again until there was no taste left in them at all. Bret shuddered at the thought of how little the tea ration was when we were planning our week on rations, he can drink tea for England and beyond.

A note on sweets. I am sure children of the 1940s had to have a lot more self-control than children today. I measured out the sweet ration, which filled a jam-jar, to show children of today how much they were entitled per month and they were horrified.

Dried Eggs

One box of dried eggs per person was allowed per month. Dried eggs were simply fresh eggs with all of the moisture removed and one box was the equivalent of twelve fresh eggs.

One tablespoons of dried egg was used as a substitute for 1 fresh egg and could be rehydrated with two tablespoons of water.

It was always a dilemma in wartime whether to use a precious fresh egg or resort to using dried eggs. Fresh eggs tasted nicer, but dried eggs lasted longer.

They do make splendid scrambled eggs and we did a taste test, Bret truly could not taste the difference.

Dried eggs were perfect for baking and when used in cakes there was no need to hydrate them before putting into the cake mixture (although I find that more moisture needs to go into the cake mixture otherwise it makes for a very heavy cake).

You can find dried eggs on Amazon and they are used a lot in the catering trade. I am quite sure you will have eaten products containing dried eggs and never known it.

Off Ration

Not everything was rationed. Fruit and veg, including potatoes, were available but only in season, so no strawberries at Christmas. Many of the exotic fruits, such as bananas, oranges, lemons and pineapple, which were available before the war, suddenly became extremely short or indeed non-existent.

My Dad, who was a child in the war, tells a story that he did not see a banana until the war was over and then did not know what to do with it when he got hold of one.

Often when oranges got into the shops they were reserved for children and invalids.

Other vegetables were also in short supply from time to time, onions being one of them and it is recorded that a single onion was raffled in the offices of The Times newspaper, which fetched a princely sum of £4.

Bread was not rationed during the war, but strangely it was rationed after the war. The Labour Government in 1946 decided to ration bread as a means of controlling the demand, it was a very unpopular decision, vehemently opposed by Churchill and the Conservatives and only lasted two years.

I do not, as a rule, mention rationing after the war, it is enough of a task to get your head around the war years, but I thought it pertinent in this case.

Fish was also not rationed, but with our fishing fleet in peril in the North Sea, fish was very hard to come by. Fishing trawlers were requisitioned for mine sweeping and to help hunt down German U-boats. So you can imagine that when a fishmonger got hold of some fish the queues went round the block.

Reading Co-Operative Society
LIMITED

Fish is Scarce !

or supplies are short, with prospects for the immediate future doubtful.

FISH ROLL

Provides an addition to the War-Time Menu.

READY TO SERVE
AND WE HAVE GOOD SUPPLIES.

Per Tin — 1/-   Sliced — per 1/8 lb.

FISH ROLL IS FREE OF "POINTS!"

To help, often river fish were sold such as perch, bream or pike. Not as lovely as Cod, I grant you, and sometimes had a strange muddy taste, but if there was nothing else, you would be grateful I am sure.

Sausages were available, however these were not sausages as we know them today, juicy delights full of flavour.

1940s sausages had very little meat content and were often stuffed more with breadcrumbs than meat. Sometimes unscrupulous butchers would even use sawdust to pack them out. Even so, sausages were scarce and in high demand.

Game was available and not rationed, so if you lived in the country and friendly with the local gamekeeper or poacher you would have been okay.

An interesting fact is that you could send game through the post, all that was required was that it was clearly and properly labelled (often the label just tied to its legs or neck).

I do wonder how our lovely posties would cope with bunnies being sent like this today!

Offal was a weekly staple; liver, kidneys, hearts, brains, pig's heads and trotters were all in high demand, no part of an animal was wasted.

A pig's head was prized and brought home to be boiled for hours, every scrap of meat was removed and brawn made from the meat and aspic. I have included the recipe later on in the book if you fancy a go.

You could eat it, but would you want to?

The Government tried some pretty unusual things to appeal to the British public and to stretch out our rations. Some became firm favourites and others definitely not.

Just after the war the food situation was dire and the Government tried to introduce Whale meat. It was not considered nice and had to be cooked for hours, then covered with a strong sauce to be even vaguely palatable.

Horse meat, although popular in France, did not catch on here, but still there were great queues for it when it was available, hungry people will eat anything.

Snoek (Barracuda), a big fish imported from South Africa, had a taste so nasty that even cats would not eat it. In fact, after the war there were so many tins of the stuff left over it was marketed as food for cats and kittens and still they would not eat it.

Later in the war Spam arrived from the USA and became a firm favourite, still seen in all leading supermarkets today and one of the classic sketches from Monty Python.

The Points System

The Points System was introduced to ration imported non-perishable goods such as dried fruit, biscuits, breakfast cereals, tinned meat and tinned fish. You got a book with points coupons, similar to ration books, and it worked in the same way as ration books. Each person had 16 points per month.

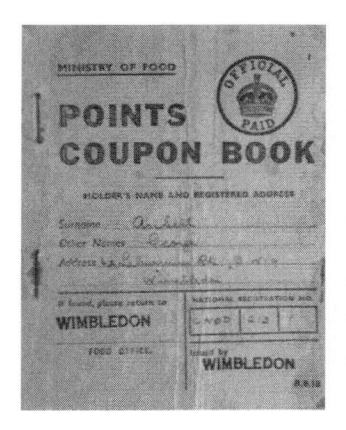

The number of points per item changed monthly, depending on supply and demand, so if suddenly a shipment of tinned tuna arrived in our ports the number of points required was reduced or if demand for Spam outweighed supply then the number of points would go up. A monthly bulletin was published in the leading newspapers with changes to the number of points for certain items. The following gives you an idea of how many points were required:

Per 1lb	Points
Tinned Fish	16-32*
Tinned Meat	16
Luncheon Meat	16
Tinned Fruit	8
Baked Beans	4
Golden Syrup or Treacle	4
Dried Fruit	8

Biscuits (chocolate)	8
Rolled Oats	2
Breakfast Cereal	4

* This would depend on the quality of fish, for example a tin of tuna would be 16 points, fine red salmon would be 32 points.

Although you could not save up your points, you could use them to store foods for special occasions. Many women used them to buy luxuries such as tinned salmon for birthdays and the favourite was to use points to buy dried fruit to make the Christmas pudding and Christmas cake.

Breaking the Law

Food in wartime was a serious business. Long queues and scarcity of food led to the black market. The cost of food on the black market was high and the cost of being caught even  higher, a hefty fine or even a prison sentence for both those selling and buying.

Wasting food was also a crime and again carried fines or in repeated cases of misdemeanour a prison sentence. The Ministry of Food even distributed posters saying that wasting food was helping Hitler, serious stuff indeed.

Don't take more than you can eat

FOOD IS A WEAPON

DON'T WASTE IT !
BUY WISELY - COOK CAREFULLY - EAT IT ALL

FOLLOW THE NATIONAL WARTIME NUTRITION PROGRAM

Dig for Victory

During World War I the Government encouraged people to plant vegetables in allotments and these became very popular, but their popularity waned after the war and many allotments fell fallow. The War Agricultural Executive Committees (known as War Ags) were formed to oversee

not only the production of home grown produce but farms and smallholdings as well. They were disbanded after the Great War.

With World War II under way, new initiatives had to be brought in to encourage the British public to feed themselves. In October 1939 the Government introduced the Grow More Food campaign, encouraging men, women and children to dig up their gardens, sports fields and take on allotments to grow their own vegetables. It was said that a small allotment could keep a family of five in vegetables for nine months of the year.

grow your own vegetables

FOR NEXT WINTER

You mustn't rely on others

On the day war was declared the War Ags were re-formed, giving them even more power than the Great War. It was their job to liaise between central Government and the growers to ensure the maximum productivity from the land.

Thousands of leaflets were distributed giving folk information such as how to prepare the land, what to grow and when.

The War Ags, although well-meaning, sometimes experienced resistance from more experienced growers. These were often older folk who resented being told how they should tend their crops from people, they thought, who had never picked up a spade.

The Grow More Food campaign was not very successful and had a mixed reception. For the first few months of the war basically nothing much happened on the Home Front, no bombs fell, no invasion happened, it was called the Phoney War. People were not aware of any food shortages, they did not see the necessity for digging up their gardens and life continued as normal.

The Government brought in the help of the newspapers in Fleet Street, London to publicise the campaign and after massive press coverage in 1941 it officially became the Dig for Victory campaign that everybody knows about today. The result of the publicity was a spectacular success as lawns and flower beds were turned over to potatoes, cabbages and all sorts of fruit and vegetables. Sportsmen were a little

more reluctant to turn over their football and cricket pitches, but eventually everyone jumped on board with Dig for Victory fever.

A short time later the Ministry of Agriculture decided that help was needed. Many people had no experience of how to grow vegetables, the right time to sow, how to tend the seedlings and when crops were ready to be picked, so more leaflets were produced and information films run in the local cinemas.

Soon the whole nation was Digging for Victory, every woman, man and child, and bumper crops produced. Even the moat of the Tower of London was planted and the Beefeaters went to work on their Dig for Victory gardens.

Children often finished school at mid-day and spent the afternoons tending crops, picking hedge-row fruits or helping their mothers and grandmothers to preserve their bounty.

Many a housewife spent so long on their allotments that dinners were late and housework neglected as they said time ran away from them and troubles were often forgotten with simple toil on the land. I can sort of understand this, even with our simple 'garden' on the boat, which just consists of some planters and tubs with flowers and herbs, a couple of hours just tending the garden in the sunshine makes you feel so much better.

CARROTS
keep you healthy and help you
to see in the blackout

Livestock

One Rabbit
has at least 12 young in a year – 45 lbs of meat

– and it's off the ration

As well as digging up their gardens it was very popular to keep livestock. Not cows and sheep as you would think of livestock, but chickens and rabbits.

My Mum told stories of having to go out and collect eggs from the hens they kept in their back garden when she was only 5 years old, a job that she absolutely hated as the hens seemed to delight in pecking her small hands.

When the hens were past their laying lives they then ended up on the table with a good selection of vegetables from the garden.

Pig Clubs

The Government recognised that for many years small-holders kept pigs, so they encouraged the practice by asking people to form pig clubs. The clubs were made up of a collective of people, perhaps from their workplace or a community and were not limited to the countryside, many pig clubs were set up in towns.

Members of the club would produce scraps for the pig to eat. When the pig was big enough, it would be slaughtered and the members got half of the pig for their own consumptions, the other half went to the Government to feed the country.

The Small Pig Keeper's Council were the national body who regulated pig clubs and they were meticulous in their duty, keeping track of the pigs so that none slipped through the net, or so they thought. Many times piglets were hidden from the inspectors and brought up to feed the pig club members alone.

Hay Box Cooking

So, what is a Hay Box? Well, to be frank, it is a box filled with hay! No, I do not mean to the flippant, it really is just a box filled with hay, although perhaps a little more complicated than that, but not much more.

It was a fantastic way of cooking a pot of food using no fuel, which was in short supply and the Government encouraged saving fuel whenever possible. Actually the hay box was the grandmother of our modern slow cookers, a way of gently cooking a pot of food long and slow.

Making a Hay Box

First you need to decide how many people you are cooking for. If it is just one person the box need only take one pot, but if you are cooking for a couple or family the box needs to be able to hold two or even three pots. We found it useful to find the pot first then build the hay box to house the pot.

Choose a square box large enough to take the pot(s) and ample room around them for padding.

The wartime books recommended a packing case, but as these are not made from wood these days they would be too flimsy. The box should have a hinged or a snug fitting lid. Bret actually made our hay box out of a pallet.

Line the box with layers of newspaper, about 15-20 layers thick and fasten to the sides of the box with drawing pins. Take a woollen blanket and line the box, again fastening it in place with drawing pins or nails.

Place about 5 inches (127mm) of sweet hay (the sort you get for pets is perfect) on the bottom the pack the box firmly with hay, making a nest in the middle for the pot to sit in.

Finally take a pillowcase and stuff it firmly with hay, this is to fit on the top.

Hay Box Cooking

The secret of hay box cooking is to get the food as piping hot as you possible can before putting the pot in the box.

Make your one pot meal and get it started on the stove top, make sure it is boiling hot before putting the lid on. Wrap the whole pot in newspaper and put it in the snug little nest you have created in the hay box. Cover the pot with the pillow case stuffed with straw, making sure it fits snugly then put the lid down on the hay box.

The amount of time needed varies a bit, but this timetable is taken from the wartime book Food Facts on the Kitchen Front:

	On the stove top	In the Hay-box
Vegetable Soups	45 minutes	4 hours
Potato or root vegetable soups	15 minutes	1 ¼ hours
Plain meat stew	30 minutes	3 ½ hours
Oatmeal porridge	45 minutes	6 hours or overnight
Stewed rice	2-3 minutes	2 ½ hours
Stewed dried fruit	2-3 minutes	3 ½ hours
Stewed fresh fruit	2-3 minutes	1 ½ hours
Suet pudding	30 minutes (boiling)	2 ½ hours

A Week on Rations

Preparation

We did not enter into our week on rations lightly, hundreds of hours of research went into it before we even opened a ration book and of course there were things that we could not do, either because the original ingredients were not  available or simply because I could not bring myself to do it (making brawn from a pig's head being one of them).

We decided to live on rations for a week, after all a day was no time at all, anyone could do it for a day. We had heard of some folk who permanently live as if in the 1940s, but this was a step too far for us so we agreed on a week – both of us were of fuller figures and therefore neither of us would actually starve to death in a week, in fact we could do with losing a bit of weight.

I am not a squeamish person, I will honestly try anything once, such as the time Bret brought home whole uncooked octopuses as they were a bargain in Tesco. I do not shy away from gutting fish or preparing any meat, but there are some things I would only do if I was literally starving, like skinning bunnies or boiling a sheep's head, so some of the recipes were either ruled out or adapted, ie I would happily buy a bunny, skinned, beheaded and ready for the pot.

You may gather from this that Bret and I are confirmed meat eaters, but in fact we have many meat-free meals. Vegetarians did rather well in the war as they had more cheese and milk than their meat-eating friends. It makes sense, in the war years meat was very sparse so lots of meals were meat-free by necessity.

We already had some 1940s cookbooks, but Bret trawled eBay for more and before long we were drowning in a sea of books, telling us everything from how to save money and coupons to how to cook a pig's head.

Before I launch into what we did, I have to say that we have done extensive research both for this book and for our displays and talks. The recipes we use are all original wartime ones, the amount and type of food we ate is exactly the same that they would have had at the time.

You may find modern books which claim to be wartime recipes but be warned if it includes 6 eggs for a cake or prime fillet steak, it is unlikely to be a genuine wartime recipe.

This is an honest account of our research, our week on rations, how we felt and what we discovered - not only about wartime rationing but about ourselves.

We decided on basic rules for our week on rations; no gadgets were to be used, no microwave, mixer, or internet for looking up recipes. No cheating, absolutely no cheating.

We decided a date to start on a misty and murky Monday in October. Why this date? Well, it seemed as good a time as any. We had nothing else on and as we could not bring ourselves to subject our friends to our self-imposed rationing experiment, decided not to entertain for the week, although many of our friends are wartime re-enactors and would probably have liked it.

On the Saturday before our week on rations I finalised the menu for the week and on Sunday we went to the shops and bought all we would need. Shopping for our week was not as straightforward as we thought, we certainly could not get everything we needed at a supermarket and had to visit a number of farm shops and small retailers to buy our ingredients.

This in itself gave us a taste of wartime living, there were no supermarkets then and such a lot of time was spent queueing at individual shops to get your weekly food. We did not have to queue but still it took an extraordinary amount of time.

If you want to follow our week and do it yourself a shopping list is at the back of the book and we have listed alternatives if you are not able to get certain ingredients.

When visiting one farm shop I asked a young lad at the meat counter where I could find brawn, he directed me to the freezer section, which I thought was odd and arriving at the freezer realised he thought I had asked for prawns! It was only when I asked a rather mature assistant that I was directed to the cold meats counter. It appears that younger folk have no idea what brawn is! By the way if you are not sure, it is a pig's head boiled for hours, all the meat removed then set in aspic. Totally delicious.

This tale was not unusual in our search for items, we were met with odd looks when asking for rabbit, pigs trotters and Camp coffee. I do wonder if the sales assistant thought I was being rather politically incorrect asking for Camp coffee, no disrespect to our LGBT friends.

We were allowed to shop during the week if absolutely necessary, but it seemed prudent to make sure we were prepared and not tempted to go off-piste.

Once back home we meticulously weighed and measured our rationed ingredients. Bret drew a big breath at the miniscule amount of cheese and tea, this is a man who loves cheese, I mean he really loves cheese, so this was going to be a big sacrifice.

We took the vegetables in season seriously as well and were lucky enough to be given some Quinces from a friendly local. I had never had anything to do with Quinces before, apart from eating pre-made quince jelly with stilton cheese - delicious, but how hard can it be, it's only a fruit isn't it?

The following is an inventory of what we had (2 people, 1 week):

Butter	4oz (114g)
Margarine	8oz (228g)
Cooking Fat	8oz (228g)
Eggs	Fresh: 2 - Dried: ½ a box
Bacon	8oz (228g)
Cheese	4oz (114g)
Milk	6 pints (3L)
Sugar	1lb (454g)
Meat	8oz (228g) sausage meat
Jam	8oz (228g)
Tea	4oz (114g)

Fruit and Vegetables

Potatoes	Carrots	Leeks
Onions	Swede	Cabbage
Cauliflower	Parsnips	Turnips
Tomatoes	Quince	Apples
Pears	Parsley	

Store Cupboard

The 1940s housewife was encouraged to keep a proper store cupboard so that meals could be conjured up at a moment's notice.

The following is what we included in our store cupboard:

Oats	Carnation Milk
Tinned Tuna	Spam
Custard Powder	Tin Peach Slices
Bisto Powder	Flour
Salt	Oxo Cubes
Tin Cod Roe	Camp Coffee
Dried Yeast	Honey
Salt	Pepper

TOO PRECIOUS TO WASTE!

Now, more than ever before, you must be *sure* of avoiding dishes that are 'failures'. McDougall reliability is vital in your cookery success. Always use McDougall's for your war-time recipes—and you will never have disasters!

Mc Dougall's

THE SELF-RAISING FLOUR THAT GIVES SURE RESULTS

The National Wheatmeal Loaf

One of the staples of food in WWII was the famous, or infamous, National Loaf, dubbed 'Hitler's Secret Weapon'. Before the war white bread was the favourite, but as the U-boats cut off our supply of wheat from abroad, white flour became scarce. The Ministry of Food, in its wisdom, introduced the Wheatmeal  Loaf in 1942, which was subsequently called 'The National Loaf'.

This was a bit like the wholemeal bread we get today but with all the wheat grain and husks included for good measure. It made a heavy bread and its dirty grey colour and gritty texture did nothing to endear itself to the public, but food was food and anything that filled you up was to be tolerated. The bread sold in shops had vitamins and minerals added to it.

An alternative for home bakers was called the Emergency Loaf, basically the same as the National Loaf, but without the additives.

Now, I am no baker. I am a fairly good cook but there's something about baking that eludes me. I could not even successfully master a bread maker many years ago, which eventually went to a car boot in disgust. So going into Rations Week I realised that I could not just pop into Tesco's and ask for a National Loaf, I would have to make my own. At this point, dear reader, all the sympathy you can muster must go to Bret for it was he who had to eat this delicacy.

The Emergency Loaf
Makes one 2 lb. loaf

1 ½ lb. wholemeal bread flour
1 tablespoon salt
1 tablespoon dried yeast
1 teaspoon honey or treacle
½ pint tepid water

Mix together all the ingredients and knead for about 10 minutes until you have a soft dough. Place the dough in an oiled bowl, cover with a damp tea towel, and leave until dough has doubled in size (around 2 hours).

Knock back the dough, give a short knead then place in an oiled loaf tin, allow to rise for a further 2 hours.

Pre-heat oven to 200°C (400° F) then bake loaf for 40-50 mins. To test the loaf, turn it out of the tin and give the base a tap; if it sounds hollow, it is ready.

Allow to cool on a wire rack

So there you have it, sounds easy and I am sure to those of you who are dedicated to the *Great British Bake Off*, it is. However, this was my experience the first time making an Emergency Loaf:

Okay, I gathered all of the ingredients.

Knead for 10 minutes! I swear my arms had not done this amount of exercise for years. After 8 minutes they could take no more, so I duly covered the beast up and waited for the stated 2 hours. I was delighted that it had doubled in size. I knocked it back, put it in the tin, whispered encouraging things to it and waited.

I think it must have objected to the knocking back as it no longer seemed inclined to rise again, but after 2 hours I thought 'sod it' and put it in the oven anyway.

Somehow I could not concentrate on anything else. This thing had taken all morning and I was sitting in front of the oven like a contender of the *Great British Bake Off*.

50 minutes later it was very brown on top but was still as miserably flat as when I put it in the oven. When I tried to get it out of the tin, it occurred to me that I forgot to grease the tin beforehand so had to resort to levering it out with a knife. It landed on the work-surface with a loud thud which did not bode well.

At this stage can I ask if you have ever seen the film *About a Boy*? The Hugh Grant character is befriended by a boy called Marcus, whose Mum has mental health problems and bakes him some bread to feed to the ducks. Marcus throws the bread in to the pond, it is so brick-like it kills a duck. Well, dear reader – I baked THAT loaf! You could build houses with this bread and never has the nickname 'Hitler's Secret Weapon' been so true.

5 hours! 5 flaming hours of my life that I will never get back, that disgusting object took! Did I give up and get one from Tesco? Well, who would know I cheated and who would blame me? I would know and I am made of sterner stuff so loaf number one went in the bin and I started again. Loaf number two came out miraculously perfect.

My Grams, my Mum's Mum, was a wonderful baker, sadly I did not inherit her skills, but I remember that she always had uncut bread. She would butter the end then cut the thinnest slices you have ever seen. This slice of bread was so delicate it was perfection in itself. I have also not inherited this skill from her and my slices could only be described as wonky doorsteps.

I mention this only because a loaf of bread cut into doorsteps really does not last long at all and after day one, to my horror, I realised that I would have to bake every other day. Fortunately, all other loaves during our week on rations turned out okay and I developed muscles in my arms I never knew I had.

Rations Week - Day One

Menu

Breakfast: A slice of Emergency Loaf with jam and cup of tea

Mid-morning coffee: made with Camp

Lunch: Spam sandwiches with a tomato

Dinner: Wartime Cauliflower Cheese

Day one of our week on rations dawned and we were up and raring to go. To give our experiment a little more kudos we decided to use original 1940s crockery as well as a splendid tea pot found on eBay.

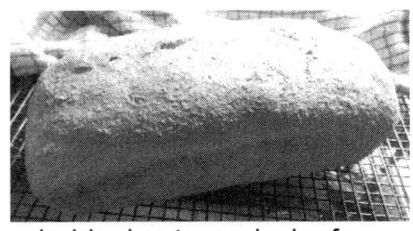

The Emergency Loaf turned out surprisingly well and was very tasty, a bit denser than normal brown bread, but that was probably due to my lack of baking skills. The tea was a bit hit and miss as we were not used to loose leaf tea, but Bret got better at tea making as the day went on.

We were very conscious of not wasting anything and that all we had would have to last a week.

I love coffee, but to keep in with the 1940s theme we found we could actually buy Camp coffee from Tesco. It is sold in a bottle and is a mixture of chicory and coffee. I remember my grandparents having it, although I was too young to be allowed it, oh lucky me! This time I tried it and it was way too sweet for my taste, although Bret thought it tolerable. It was to be my first and last experience of Camp coffee, I would stick to tea from then on.

I actually like Spam and a nice sandwich with a thin smear of butter and a bit of Spam was really okay, I even managed to slice the loaf so it resembled slices and not ungainly wedges of bread. We decided to eke out our Spam, so only used half of the tin, it did make the sandwiches a bit sparse, but I added some sliced tomato and it was not too bad.

Oh dear, oh dear, oh dear! The wartime cauliflower cheese was really not good at all, if I had not known our precious ration of cheese in it I would never have guessed. We even used up a couple of our rashers of bacon to try and cheer it up but to no avail. It did, however, really bring home to us the sort of meals people had to eat during the war.

An interesting point to note that during the war all parts of a vegetable were used so when preparing the cauliflower I included the leaves, which are normally thrown away today.

If I had not known it had cheese in it and was doing a blind taste test, I would never have known and the sauce was a bit thin, but with carrots, lots of parsley and a slice of bread and butter, it was filling and passable.

We made it to the end of day one. My main concern was that we would run out of milk by the end of the week, 6 pints sounds a lot, but it was going down very quickly.

Wartime Cauliflower Cheese

1 fresh cauliflower
2 tablespoons cornflour
½ pint milk
1 onion or 1 leek
2 oz cheese
Salt and pepper
Horseradish or mustard
Knob of butter (optional)

Steam or boil the cauliflower and then drain well and put into an oven-proof dish. Fry leek or onion and put aside.

Make the sauce; mix the cornflour with a little of the milk until it forms a thick paste. Add the rest of the milk and knob of butter if using.

Place on the heat and slowly bring to a simmer stirring all the time, lower heat and add in salt & pepper, a little horseradish or dried mustard. Add the leeks or onions then pour over the cauliflower. Grate the cheese and sprinkle over the top. Place under the grill until browned.

Rations Week - Day Two

Menu

Breakfast: A slice of the Emergency Loaf with jam and cup of tea

Lunch: Vegetable Soup and a slice of bread and butter

Dinner: Woolton Pie, Cabbage and Gravy

Breakfast was the usual, bread, a smear of butter and jam with a cup of Bret's now delicious tea. We were really being stingy with our tea leaves and re-using them until the tea resembled gnat's pee, but were worried about running out.

I spent most of the morning baking another loaf, cutting up root vegetables for the soup and pie and washing up. Heaven alone knows how the women in the war found time to do a job and war work, perhaps they were just a lot more organised than me.

The soup was delicious, packed with root vegetables and plenty of flavour. Accompanied by the bread it was very filling and no need for anything else.

Vegetable Soup

This has got to be the easiest recipe in the world. Take a selection of vegetables, whatever you have got, such as carrots, potatoes, leeks, onions, turnips, swede, etc. Peel and chop evenly, all about the same size. Put in a pan with vegetable stock and water and boil until soft. At this stage you can either leave the vegetables whole or mash them to make a smooth soup. Season with salt and pepper, sprinkle with parsley, eat and enjoy.

Dinner was a triumph, Lord Woolton Pie, named after the Minister for Food. If you try nothing else from this book, try this.

The first task was to make the potato pastry, it is like shortcrust but the mashed potato makes it very moist. For the pie you simply simmer the vegetables in a little Marmite (or Vegemite if you prefer), add some oats and lots of parsley, cover with the pastry and put it in the oven until the pastry is cooked. So simple and absolutely scrummy, I was even impressed with my pastry, which melted in the mouth.

Lord Woolton Pie

(Food Facts)

1 lb. of diced root vegetables (whatever is in season such as potatoes, swede, carrots and cauliflower)
3 or 4 spring onions
1 teaspoon vegetable extract
1 tablespoon oatmeal

Cook together for 10 minutes with just enough water to cover. Stir occasionally to stop from sticking.
Allow to cook and put into a pie dish, sprinkle with a little parsley and cover with potato pastry.

Potato Pastry

(Food Facts)

8 oz. sieved, cooked potatoes
4 oz. flour
½ teaspoon salt
2 oz. cooking fat

Adding mashed potato makes for a very filling and moist pastry.

Sieve the flour with the salt. Rub the fat into the flour until it resembles breadcrumbs. Add the potato and mix to a dry dough (add a little water if necessary). Roll out and use for either sweet or savoury dishes.

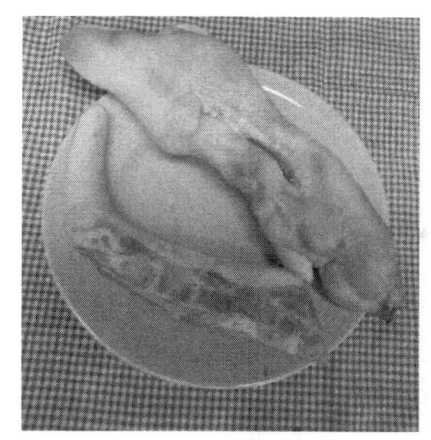 Bret went shopping and came home beaming as he procured a pig's trotter and tail from the local butcher, he went in and told him what we were doing and was presented with these, free. I am sure that housewives in the war would have been delighted, but this is not the first odd present I have been given to cook and I'm sure will not be the last.

I spent the evening looking through the 1940s cookery books for how to cook my 'presents' and decided to put the deed off until later in the week. This is where the Internet is so handy, but was banned for this week.

Day 2 was a good day, the soup and evening meal were very filling and we certainly did not go to bed hungry. The milk ration was holding up well and we felt we had not wasted anything.

Tip: Cook extra vegetables for the evening meal to be used for Bubble and Squeak the next day.

Rations Week - Day Three

Menu

Breakfast: Porridge
Lunch: Tinned cod's roe on toast with tomato
Dinner: Spam fritters, bubble and squeak and carrots
Apple crumble and custard

The porridge for breakfast was delicious, made with water, just a little of our milk ration and a sprinkling of sugar. It was certainly filling and set us up for the day ahead.

Lunch was lovely, both of us had grown up having roe on toast. Fresh roe is a bit strange to prepare, there are not very many places that sell it, but is completely  delicious to eat. We had the tin of roe from our store cupboard, spread it on the toast and grilled it for a few minutes. With plenty of salt and vinegar it was not as good as the fresh roe but still very tasty.

Dinner used up the rest of the Spam from our lunch on Day One, batter was made using one spoon of dried eggs (the equivalent of 1 egg – If you can't get hold of any dried eggs (available on Amazon) cheat and use an additional fresh egg), flour and water and they were fried in lard. Perhaps not the most appealing objects, but there's a war on, don't you know!

Bubble and Squeak was a wartime favourite for using up left-over vegetables and certainly in my family we had it every Monday with the vegetables left over from the Sunday roast. It is so simple to make, just take your left-over veg, put them in a frying pan with a little lard and fry until crispy, indeed the crispy bits are always the best in my opinion. Today you can use vegetable oil, but it's not half as tasty as using lard or even beef dripping.

It still seemed to take ages to make the simplest of things. Of course I was not using modern appliances apart from oven and hob - no microwave, bread maker or food processor for me that week and I could appreciate how they speed things up.

Rations seemed to be holding up well,

Apple Crumble and Custard

Apples (peeled, cored and chopped)
Self-raising flour
Butter or margarine
Oats (optional)
Sugar to taste
Bird's Custard

Place the apples in an oven-proof dish. If using cooking apples sweeten with a little sugar.

Rub the fat into the flour then add the oats if using.

Dot fat over the top and place in a pre-heated oven until the apple is cooked and the topping browned.

In wartime housewives used Birds Custard whenever possible as it saved on eggs and sugar.

Rations Week - Day Four

Menu

Breakfast: Bread Pudding
Lunch: Brawn on toast
Dinner: Rabbit stew with dumplings, cabbage and
parsnips
Tinned peaches and Carnation milk

Bread pudding for breakfast, how scrumptious is that! Juicy, spicy and filling, it was a staple of life in WWII.

Bread pudding has always been a family favourite. This recipe was actually a treasured

one by my Grams (Mum's Mum) and was a closely guarded secret in the family. As testament to how close Grams and my Dad were, she left the recipe to him in her will and now it has passed down to me. Of course if you look at lots of wartime recipes for bread pudding they are all similar, but by using this particular one I can imagine her cooking it and it makes me feel close to her once again.

Of course it used up our two precious eggs, it was a serious decision, but the thing about bread pudding is that it is very filling so you only need a little at a time to satisfy you.

Bread Pudding

(Family Recipe)

    16oz. Bread (preferably stale)
    4oz. Suet (either beef or vegetable)
    12oz. Sultanas
    2oz. Soft Brown Sugar
    2 level teaspoon Mixed Spice
    2 level teaspoon Cinnamon
    2 tablespoon Golden Syrup
    2 Eggs

Tear up the bread and put it in a bowl with just enough water to soak it.
Leave until the bread is soft then squeeze out as much of the liquid as possible (this is most important and is the difference between a firm lovely bread pudding and a soggy mush).
Mix in all of the other ingredients thoroughly.
Place in a tin which has been greased.
Bake in the oven at 160° for 1½ - 2 hours, checking occasionally (if the top is looking too brown cover with a sheet of greaseproof paper).
Sprinkle the top with a little sugar

Right, now I have a confession to make, I cheated. I did not make my own Brawn. Firstly I could not get a pig's head – not that I tried too hard, and secondly we  could not afford the gas for cooking it for hours (we cook on bottled gas) and thirdly I just didn't fancy it. Tracking down Brawn to buy was not easy but I eventually found it at a farm shop. It was delicious, firm and chunky bits of ham in a lovely aspic jelly, I really enjoyed it and will be having it again post rations week. I have included the recipe if you fancy having a go, but I would not blame you if not.

Brawn

½ pig's head or sheep's head
Bouquet of herbs
½ lb shin of beef
3 cloves
2-3 peppercorns
Get the butcher to clean the head for you. Soak it overnight. Steam the beef, herbs, peppercorns and cloves, cover then boil until the meat completely falls off the bones. Remove the lid and boil until the liquid is reduced. Remove the bones. Mash up the meat and fat, adding a little stock to moisten.

Press into moulds and leave to set. Skim off the fat from the remaining liquid. The liquid is good for soup.

Another sort of cheat… The story goes like this… A bunny jumped nto my basket as I walked through a field that we were moored next tc! That's the story we are sticking to should the local Bobby ask.

Actually I boucht said bunny (skinned and chopped up ready to cook) from the same farm shop where I got the brawn.

I like rabbit, it tastes a bit like chicken, but has lots of little bones which are a pain and it takes ages to cook, Nice thick herby dumplings added to the stew made it really filling, a real comfort food.

We decided tc try out our hay box for the stew so the rabbit was soaked the night before (as per the recipe) and ithe stew had to be made early in the morning to give it time to cook. Of course if you are trying this you don't have to make a hay box, just cook it in the oven. First I got it all prepared and the stew to bciling temperature, then I put the lid firmly on, Bret wrapped it in newspaper and placed the pot in the nest we had created in the hay box, covered it with the pillow case stuffed with hay and firmly put the lid down.

There was a temptation to open the box and see how the stew was doing, but I resisted as letting the heat out would defeat the task.

When it came to dinner time opening the hay box was akin to opening an elaborately wrapped present at Christmas, full of anticipation. Would we like the contents? Would we be disappointed and end up with a cold, inedible mess?

We both opened the lid, removed the pillow case and delved down into the hay box to carefully lift out our prize.

It was warm and definitely well cooked. We did have to heat it up again, but actually the results were very good and of course it used no power at all.

Rabbit Stew

Cut the rabbit into neat joints. Soak them for 12 hours in a marinade of vinegar 1 part and cider 2 parts, bay leaves, thyme, rosemary, fennel, salt and pepper. Drain the rabbit, dry and brown in a liberal amount of butter with a little onion. Place in a casserole. Work 2 tablespoons of flour into the butter in which the rabbit was fried, brown it, mix smoothly with a little water, boil and pour over the rabbit and add water if required. Simmer until tender then add, if liked, a tablespoon of gooseberry or redcurrant jelly.

Pudding was a real treat, tinned peaches and Carnation milk. To have this in the 1940s would have meant saving up coupons and you would probably only have this for special occasions or at Christmas.

This brought back memories from my childhood of Sunday tea and we had tinned fruit salad and Carnation milk the prize was to get the one half a cherry in the tin.

We felt that day four was a really good one, plenty of filling food, full of flavour. I still felt that I spent the whole day cooking, washing up, preparing food, cooking and washing up.

This week on rationing felt like a full-time job, and if I was not retired and had to do actual work it would have been quite impossible.

Rations Week - Day Five

Menu

Breakfast: Porridge with a splodge of jam
Morning: Bovril
Lunch: Cabbage and left over bunny stew
Dinner: Fish and chips
Apple and pear Betty

Today was the best, starting with porridge and a splodge of our rationed jam was filling and lovely.

In the morning we had a hot drink of Bovril. I had actually forgotten how nice this is as a hot drink and made a great change from tea, having given up hope of having a nice coffee all week.

Lunch was all about using up left-overs and not wasting anything.

Dinner, oh how I loved this – fish and chips from the chip shop. With both potatoes and fish off-ration the chip shop was probably more popular in the 1940s than it is today. However, it was not open all the time and depended on the chippie getting hold of fish. When the sought-after fish was available he put a sign in the window 'frying tonight'.

Massive queues formed early on in eager anticipation of getting the prized fish and chips and I can only imagine how devastating it was to reach the head of the queue only to be told they had run out.

Fortunately we did not have to queue for more than a few minutes, they did not run out and I cannot tell you how much I savoured every mouthful of those salt and vinegar chips, crisp batter and soft white fish.

We followed our feast with Apple and Pear Betty, with both apples and pears plentiful, the Betty with thick custard finished off our meal a real treat.

Apple and Pear Betty

1 ½ lbs apples and pears
2 oz butter
1 gill water
Grated rind of 1 lemon
2 tablespoon sugar
2 tablespoon golden syrup
6 oz breadcrumbs
¼ teaspoon cinnamon
¼ teaspoon nutmeg

Butter a pie dish. Mix lemon rind with spices and crumbs. Core and slice apples and pears into a basin. Place a layer of fruit in the pie dish covered with a layer of crumbs. Dab with dots of butter. Repeat layers until all crumbs and fruit have been used up. Put the water and syrup into

a saucepan and heat until combined, pour over the crumbs and fruit. Sprinkle with sugar and dot with remaining butter.
Place in a pan with and inch of water and cook in the middle of the oven for about 1 hour.

We did a stock check after day five, most of the rations were holding up well, plenty of sugar left, but as we don't really have a sweet tooth, that was okay. Milk had all but run out and we reverted to dried milk, certainly not as nice and I think would have been a constant problem for us in the 1940s.

We did not weigh ourselves at the start of the week, which was rather an oversight, but we had been using smaller plates than usual and felt a lot better.

Rations Week - Day Six

Menu

Breakfast: Toast and dripping
Lunch: Potato Floddies
Dinner: Pasty, leeks, carrots and jacket potato

I got up at the crack of dawn to bake yet another loaf of bread, with the thought that this one really should last us to the end of the week, then I would cheerfully never bake another one.

As I child I remember having toast and dripping, usually for Sunday tea. The dripping was made from the lard and meat juices, usually beef, and cooled until the top was lard and the bottom a thick brown jelly. Spread onto warm thick toast with a sprinkling of salt it was pure comfort food. Today we are far too health conscious to make dripping, I never cook with lard and using vegetable oil never works.

It is a great wonder that people in the 1940s were so slim with the likes of dripping and so many filling meals, but they really were tiny, very few women now would ever be able to squeeze themselves into original 1940s dresses. I can only assume it was because portion sizes were much smaller and that everyone either walked or cycled everywhere.

Wash days were hard physical work and shopping was carried in big, heavy bags. Perhaps we are too lazy or soft these days!

The story for lunch is that I got a tin of tuna from Sid the Spiv. Risking buying things on the black market was a very dodgy business with the threat of big fines or even prison, but must have been very tempting at times. Anyway Mum's the word so don't tell anyone will you.

For dinner I made the potato pastry again that I made for the Lord Woolton pie and filled it with root veg, in effect it was very similar to the pie, but just shaped as a pasty.

Our rations were going down at an alarming rate, but only one day to go. Tea was scarce and we were re-using the tea leaves until the tea tasted and looked a bit like dish water.

Potato Floddies

2 large potatoes
Flour
Seasoning
Frying Fat

Scrub the potatoes then grate them into a bowl. Add sufficient flour to form a batter (no need to add liquid). Heat a frying pan, add the frying fat and make it very hot. Drop the mixture into the pan and fry until brown then turn over and cook the other side. Herbs or a dash of cayenne pepper can be added to give more flavour or can be served plain with jam for a sweet dish.

Rations Week - Day Seven

Menu

Breakfast: Scrambled eggs on toast
Lunch: Potato soup with shredded pig's trotter
Snack: Crackling made from pig's skin, crisp potatoes and Cheese straws
Dinner: Murky, roast potatoes, parsnips cabbage and carrots
Quince crumble pie and custard

The final day!

A treat for breakfast this morning. I hydrated our remaining dried eggs and scrambled them, serving them on thick wedges of toast. Could we tell the difference between fresh scrambled eggs and dried? Actually there was very little difference.

I finally got around to cooking the pig's trotter and tail then gave Bret the job of extracting the meat from them, not a lovely job. The amount of meat produced was tiny so decided to add it to the soup for lunch. The soup was simply potato, onion and stock with the pig meat added in. It was not Cordon Bleu, but edible and filling.

Having got everything together for the last meal I decided not to waste a scrap so did a little selection of canapes (if I dare describe them as that) for pre-dinner snacks.

I used the skin from the trotter to make into crackling, covering it with salt and putting in a very hot oven until it crackled. The potato peelings were brushed with fat and roasted in the oven. Then came the piece de resistance – cheese straws, using the precious last ounce of Cheddar. Believe me dear friends, a cheese straw has never tasted as good as that one.

By now you must be wondering what Murcky was, wonder no more. In the war, especially at Christmas, turkeys were not plentiful so often they would take other meat, sometimes mincemeat but in this case I used sausage meat, and form it into the shape of a turkey. The sausage meat was mixed with onion, breadcrumbs (most often more breadcrumbs than meat), grated carrot, mashed potato and herbs then shaped into the general shape of a turkey. The name comes from Mock Turkey, hence. I do wonder about the Mock Duck, named Muck. Was it as awful as the image I conjure up?

Mock Turkey (Murkey)

(Stork Margarine)
The following recipe is good for 4 people, please adjust up or down to suit.

Sausage Meat (about 2lbs
Parsley
Mashed Potato (allow 1 potato for each person)
Breadcrumbs (approximately 3 slices)
Grated carrots
1 Egg
Bacon Rashers to cover the Murkey
2 big parsnips (peeled)
Mix together the sausage meat, cold mashed potato, parsley, egg and breadcrumbs. Season to taste.
Form the mixture into the shape of a cooked turkey or chicken, placing the parsnips either side.
Cover the Murkey with the bacon rashers.
Bake in the cover for approximately 1-1 ½ hours.

It was time to tackle the quinces and I was not too sure how to do this. Quince are tremendously hard, difficult to peel and cut and the advice from the neighbour who gave them to us was just to chop them up unpeeled and simmer them until soft then sieve away the peel and pips. I did as recommended and ended up with a pig pan of slush. The other thing with them is that they are very sour so I used the remainder of my rationed sugar to sweeten them and the whole thing was topped with left-over oats.

The custard was not very sweet, having used up all my sugar for the quince, but still on top of the crumble was lovely.

Anyway the meal was a triumph and a fitting end to our week on rations.

Rations Week Reflections

We thoroughly enjoyed our week on rations, it was fun, entertaining, thought provoking and educational. We would not want to do it permanently, but would certainly do it again. We learnt far more than just reading about rationing and what your average family went through in the war.

The thing that struck me more than anything was the amount of time everything took. No sooner than we had breakfast and washed up it was time to prepare lunch and so the day went on. Baking bread every other day was a major headache, it would have been so much easier to just go out and buy it, but thinking of the 1940s housewives they would have walked to their baker, joined a queue and waited for their turn, possibly to be told that the baker had sold out and had nothing else to offer.

I am sure they would have been more organised that I was, making sure that if they cooked potato for dinner there would be enough left over the next day to make pastry and preparing enough vegetables for a couple of days rather than doing them each day.

We both learned a lot, Bret researched and made our hay box, we both researched the food and meals and it does not stop there. There is always a new old book to scour through, a Facebook group who just focus on living on rations and give loads of ideas and tips.

Yes we will do another week, but may well give it a couple of years break while we get our fill of tea and cheese!

As for how we actually felt after our week, I can say there was no obvious weight loss or gain, but mentally we felt more alive in that we had so much to do, plan and talk about that we felt more connected. Meals were times of exploration, of tastes, textures, looks and smells, all to be talked about with suggestions for improvement or even deciding that we would never want it again!

In these days of fast food and fast living we seldom spend time thinking about what we are eating and the sheer mechanics of where our food comes from, the best way to prepare it and above all not wasting anything.

Going back to 1940s rationing has certainly made me think about the food all of us waste and has made me more conscious of how much food I actually need, which is far less than I cook and put on my plate.

So I would urge you to try it, you never know you might make major and permanent changes to your diet.

If you really can't stand the thought of eating rabbit then perhaps cheat a little and have chicken. Likewise if you can't get brawn then a tin of corned beef would do just as well.

Shopping List

If you would like to try our week on rations I have included a shopping list.

These quantities are for two people so please adjust as necessary.

Of course you do not have to stick to this, but unless you have access to 1940s cookery books it can be a long and time consuming job to work it all out so this might help. The quantities are for 2 people so please adjust them if you need to and I have included a conversion chart for those of you not used to working in imperial weights.

Dairy

Butter 4oz
Cooking Fat 8oz
Milk 6 pints

Margarine 8oz
Cheese 2oz
Fresh Eggs 2

Meat and Fish

Bacon 8oz
Sausage meat 4oz
Rabbit (1 rabbit prepared)
Spam 1 tin
Cod Roe 1 tin

Fruit and Vegetables

Cauliflower
Potatoes
Leeks
Swede
Parsnips
Quince
Pears

Tomatoes
Carrots
Onions
Cabbage
Turnips
Apples

Store Cupboard

Wholemeal Bread Flour
Yeast sachets (1 packet)
Salt
Camp Coffee
Tea 4oz
Corn Flour
Mustard
Salt and Pepper
Vegetable Stock
Parsley
Self-Raising Flour
Porridge Oats
Jam 1 jar
Bisto gravy
Sugar (1 lb)

Conversion Chart

The conversions have been rounded up or down as appropriate.

IMPERIAL	METRIC
1 oz. (ounce)	28g
2 oz.	57g
4 oz.	113g
8 oz. (half a pound)	227g
1 lb (pound)	454g
1 cup	28g
1 teaspoon	4g
1 dessertspoon	10g
1 tablespoon	15g
1 pint	568 ml
1 gill (4 fluid ounces)	

Contents

Printed in Great Britain
by Amazon